I0461752

Summary

The Troubled Asset Relief Program (TARP) was created by the Emergency Economic Stabilization Act (EESA; P.L. 110-343) in October 2008. EESA was enacted to address an ongoing financial crisis that reached near-panic proportions in September 2008. The act granted the Secretary of the Treasury authority to either purchase or insure up to $700 billion in troubled assets owned by financial institutions. This authority was granted for up to two years from the date of enactment and was very broad. In particular, the definitions of both "troubled asset" and "financial institution" allowed the Secretary wide leeway in deciding what assets might be purchased or guaranteed and what might qualify as a financial firm.

The financial crisis grew out of an unprecedented housing boom that turned into a housing bust. Much of the lending for housing during the boom was based on asset-backed securities that used the repayment of housing loans as the basis of these securities. As housing prices fell and mortgage defaults increased, these securities became illiquid and fell sharply in value, causing capital losses for firms holding them. Uncertainty about future losses reduced many firms' access to private liquidity, with the loss in liquidity being catastrophic in some cases. September 2008 saw the government takeover of Fannie Mae and Freddie Mac, the bankruptcy of Lehman Brothers, and the near collapse of AIG, which was saved only by an $85 billion loan from the Federal Reserve. There was widespread lack of trust in the financial markets as participants were unsure which firms might be holding so-called toxic assets that might now be worth much less than previously estimated, and thus might be unreliable counterparties in financial transactions. This prevented firms from accessing credit markets to meet their liquidity needs.

As EESA moved through Congress, most attention was focused on the idea of the government purchasing mortgage-related toxic assets, thus alleviating the widespread uncertainty and suspicion by cleaning up bank balance sheets. The initial TARP Capital Purchase Program, however, directly added capital onto banks' balance sheets through preferred share purchases, rather than removing assets that had become liabilities through purchasing mortgage-related assets. Several other TARP programs followed, including an asset guarantee program; programs designed to spur consumer and business lending; financial support for companies such as AIG, GM, and Chrysler; and programs to aid homeowners at risk of foreclosure. Eventually, the Public-Private Investment Program resulted in the purchase of some mortgage-related assets, but this has remained a relatively small part of TARP. Most of the TARP programs are now closed.

With the immediate crisis subsiding through 2009, congressional attention to financial services turned largely to consider broad regulatory changes. The resulting Dodd-Frank Act (P.L. 111-203) amended the TARP authority, including (1) reduction of the overall amount to $475 billion; (2) removal of the ability to reuse TARP funds that had been repaid; and (3) removal of the authority to create new TARP programs or initiatives. The original TARP authority to purchase new assets or enter into new contracts expired on October 3, 2010. Outlays under the existing contracts, however, may continue through the life of these contracts. Overall budget-cost estimates for TARP have decreased significantly since the passage of EESA, with the latest Congressional Budget Office estimates foreseeing $32 billion in costs and the latest Treasury estimates foreseeing $60 billion in costs. Most of these costs are from aid for homeowners, for the insurer AIG, and for U.S. automakers. The assistance to banks is generally showing a gain for the government. In the 112th Congress, several bills have been introduced to repeal all or part of TARP, including H.R. 189, H.R. 430, H.R. 830, H.R. 839, H.R. 1315, S. 162 and S. 527.

Contents

Tables

Appendixes

Contacts

Introduction

The Troubled Asset Relief Program (TARP) was created by the Emergency Economic Stabilization Act[1] (EESA) enacted on October 3, 2008. EESA was passed by Congress and signed by President Bush to address an ongoing financial crisis that reached near-panic proportions in September 2008.

Financial turmoil began in August 2007 when asset-backed securities, particularly those backed by subprime mortgages, suddenly became illiquid and fell sharply in value as an unprecedented housing boom turned to a housing bust. The Federal Reserve (Fed) stepped in with emergency measures to restore liquidity, temporarily calming markets. Losses in mortgage markets, however, continued and spilled into other markets. Financial firms eventually wrote down many of these losses, depleting their capital. Uncertainty about future losses on illiquid and complex assets led to some firms having reduced access to private liquidity, with the loss in liquidity being catastrophic in some cases.

September 2008 saw the government takeover of Fannie Mae and Freddie Mac, the bankruptcy of Lehman Brothers, and the near collapse of AIG, which was averted with an $85 billion loan from the Fed. There was widespread unwillingness to lend in the financial markets as participants were unsure which firms might be holding so-called toxic assets now worth much less than previously estimated, and thus might be unreliable counterparties in financial transactions.

EESA authorized the Secretary of the Treasury (hereafter "the Secretary") to either purchase or insure up to $700 billion in troubled assets owned by financial firms. This authority was granted for a maximum of two years from the date of enactment and expired on October 3, 2010. The general concept was that by removing such assets from the financial system, confidence in counterparties could be restored and the system could resume functioning. This authority granted in EESA was very broad. In particular, the definitions of both "troubled assets" and "financial institutions" allowed the Secretary wide latitude in deciding what assets might be purchased or guaranteed and what might qualify as a financial institution.[2] EESA also included a number of oversight mechanisms[3] and reporting requirements.[4] EESA was later amended to strengthen its executive compensation requirements[5] and to reduce the authorized amount to $475 billion.[6]

---

[1] P.L. 110-343, 12 U.S.C. 5311 *et seq.*

[2] The definition for financial institution gives examples, such as banks and credit unions, but specifically does not limit the definition to the types of firms named. The definition of troubled asset includes "any financial instrument" determined by the Secretary, in consultation with the Chairman of the Fed, the purchase of which would promote financial stability.

[3] See CRS Report R40099, *The Special Inspector General for the Troubled Asset Relief Program (SIGTARP)*, by Vanessa K. Burrows and CRS Report RL34713, *Emergency Economic Stabilization Act: Preliminary Analysis of Oversight Provisions*, by Curtis W. Copeland.

[4] Treasury publishes their TARP reports at http://www.treasury.gov/initiatives/financial-stability/briefing-room/reports/Pages/Home.aspx. This report will make use of many of these TARP reports. Monthly overall reports are required under Section 105(a) of EESA and will be referenced hereafter as, for example, the "December 2010 TARP 105(a) Report." Monthly reports on dividends and interest accrued to TARP will be referenced hereafter as, for example, the "December 2010 TARP Dividends and Interest Report." These reports are typically published 10 days after the month in question. Treasury also is required to publish a "TARP Transactions Report" detailing TARP transactions shortly after they occur. In 2011, Treasury began to publish a "Daily TARP Update" as well.

[5] P.L. 111-5; see CRS Report R40540, *Executive Compensation Limits in Selected Federal Laws*, by Michael V. Seitzinger and Carol A. Pettit.

This report provides a brief outline of the programs created under TARP, changes made by Congress, and a summary of the current status and estimated costs of the program. It also provides an **Appendix** that contains detailed discussions of the individual TARP programs. This report will be updated as warranted by market and legislative events.

TARP Programs

Treasury reacted quickly after the enactment of EESA, announcing the TARP Capital Purchase Program, on October 14, 2008, and several other programs followed. These programs can be broadly broken down into Bank Support Programs, Credit Market Programs, Other Programs, and Housing Programs with several programs under each of these headings:

Bank Support Programs

- **Capital Purchase Program (CPP).** The CPP did not purchase the mortgage-backed securities that were seen as toxic to the system, but instead purchased preferred shares in banks.[7] The resulting addition of capital, it was hoped, would allow banks to overcome the effect of the toxic assets while the assets remained on bank balance sheets. The CPP is now closed, with $11.6 billion outstanding, but no additional disbursements are possible under the current program.

- **Targeted Investment Program (TIP).** This program provided for exceptional preferred share purchases and was used only for Citigroup and Bank of America. This program is closed, with all funds repaid.

- **Asset Guarantee Program (AGP).** The AGP, required by Section 102 of EESA, provided guarantees that were also part of the exceptional assistance to Citigroup and Bank of America. This program is closed, with all guarantees cancelled and no funds having been actually disbursed.

- **Community Development Capital Initiative (CDCI).** The CDCI provided for lower dividend rates on preferred share purchases from banks that target their lending to small businesses. Many of the participants in the CDCI converted into the program from the CPP, This program is closed with $0.57 billion still outstanding, but no new disbursements are possible under the current program.

Credit Market Programs

- **Public-Private Investment Program (PPIP).** This program provides funds and guarantees for purchases of mortgage-related securities from bank balance sheets. Purchases and management of the securities is done by private investors who have provided capital to invest along with the TARP funds. The PPIP is still open under previous contracts with $18.0 billion of a possible $21.9 billion disbursed.

(...continued)

[6] P.L. 111-203.

[7] Preferred stock is an equity instrument, but it does not confer any control over the company and typically has a set dividend rate to be paid by the company; it is similar economically to debt, but accounted for as equity.

- **Term Asset-Backed Securities Loan Facility (TALF).** The program was operated by the Federal Reserve to support the asset-backed security market.[8] Initial losses, should their be any, however, are to accrue to TARP. To this point, no losses have occurred, although $0.1 billion was disbursed, largely to cover expenses. Up to $4.2 billion in additional disbursements are possible under TALF, but substantial disbursements are not expected.

- **Section 7(a) Securities Purchase Program.** This program supported the Small Business Administration's (SBA's) Section 7(a) loan program through purchases of pooled SBA guaranteed securities to increase credit availability for small businesses. It is now closed with no funds outstanding.

Other Programs

- **AIG Assistance (Systemically Significant Failing Institution Program).**[9] TARP preferred share purchases supplemented and ultimately supplanted assistance to AIG previously provided by the Federal Reserve. The AIG assistance was restructured in January 2011 with the government peak ownership 92% of AIG's common equity. The Treasury has begun selling this equity, with 61% remaining to be sold, but no target date has been announced for its final disposal. Outstanding is $30.4 billion, but no additional disbursements to AIG are possible under the current program.

- **Automobile Industry Support.**[10] This program initially provided loans to support General Motors (GM) and Chrysler and ultimately included preferred share purchases from the auto financing company GMAC (now renamed Ally Financial). The program ultimately resulted in majority government ownership of GM (60.8%) and GMAC/Ally Financial (74%), and minority government ownership of Chrysler (9.9%). The ownership in GM was reduced to 33.3% in a public share offering in December 2010 and currently stands at 32% with additional dilution possible due to exercise of private options. The U.S. government's ownership stake in Chrysler was sold to Fiat in May 2011. A public share offering of GMAC/Ally Financial shares was planned in the middle of 2011, but was postponed. No date for sale of the government's equity in GMAC/Ally Financial has been announced. Total outstanding is $37.1 billion, with no new disbursements possible under the current program.

---

[8] For more information, see CRS Report RL34427, *Financial Turmoil: Federal Reserve Policy Responses*, by Marc Labonte.

[9] For more detailed information on AIG, see CRS Report R40438, *Federal Government Assistance for American International Group (AIG)*, by Baird Webel.

[10] For more information, see CRS Report R41978, *The Role of TARP Assistance in the Restructuring of General Motors*, by Bill Canis and Baird Webel, CRS Report R41940, *TARP Assistance for Chrysler: Restructuring and Repayment Issues*, by Baird Webel and Bill Canis, and CRS Report R41846, *TARP Assistance for the U.S. Motor Vehicle Industry: Unwinding the Government Stake in GMAC*, by Baird Webel, Gary Shorter, and Bill Canis.

Housing Programs[11]

These programs are unlike the other TARP programs in that they do not result in valuable assets or income in return for the TARP funding. All of these programs remain open under the contracts previously agreed to and substantial funds remain to be disbursed:

- **Home Affordable Modification Program (HAMP).** HAMP pays mortgage servicers if they modify mortgages to reduce the financial burden on homeowners. A total of $29.9 billion in disbursements is possible under the program, with $2.85 billion disbursed.

- **Hardest Hit Fund (HHF).** HHF provides aid to state housing finance agency programs in states that have high unemployment rates or experienced the steepest declines in home prices. Eighteen states and the District of Columbia are participating in HHF. Of a possible $7.6 billion, $0.9 billion has been disbursed.

- **FHA Short Refinance.** This program promotes refinancing of mortgages on "underwater" properties, those on which the mortgage balance is greater than the equity in the house, if lenders agree to forgive some of the principal balance owed on the mortgages. Of a possible $8.1 billion, $0.06 billion has been disbursed.

Current Status and Future of TARP

As detailed above, until October 3, 2010, the Secretary had the authority to purchase or insure nearly any financial asset under the programs in place on June 25, 2010. This authority has expired. The legal contracts entered into under the previous authority, however, are still in force. Thus, TARP funds may still flow out from the Treasury in the future. The programs with the largest gap between legal commitments and the actual amount disbursed, and thus the largest potential to grow in the future, are the housing support programs. **Table 1** presents the figures reported by the Treasury for obligated and actually disbursed TARP funds.

Table 1. Outlay of TARP Funds
($ in billions)

TARP Program	Obligated Amount	Actual Disbursements
Bank Support Programs	$250.46	$245.10
Credit Market Programs	$26.52	$18.42
AIG	$67.84	$67.84
Auto Industry Financing Program	$79.69	$79.69
Housing Support	$45.60	$3.83
Totals	$470.12	$414.88

Source: May 15, 2012 Daily TARP Update.

Note: Figures may not sum due to rounding.

---

[11] For more information, see CRS Report R40210, *Preserving Homeownership: Foreclosure Prevention Initiatives*, by Katie Jones.

Although the total amount of assets held or insured under TARP was initially capped at $700 billion, and the program was widely reported as a "$700 billion bailout,"[12] the actual net cost of TARP was never likely to approach $700 billion. Unlike most government programs, where funds are simply expended, TARP funds were generally used in ways that resulted in either the holding of assets by the government or in some form of income accruing to the government. The incoming receipts from TARP outlays have taken several forms, including

- funds from the sale of previously purchased assets,

- repayment of principal from loans,

- premium payments for insured assets,

- dividend and interest payments from assets and loans, and

proceeds from the sale of warrants issued by companies who sold assets to TARP.

Table 2 summarizes these incoming revenues from TARP. According to EESA, revenues and proceeds from the sale of troubled assets, or from warrants and senior debt instruments, "shall be paid into the general fund of the Treasury for reduction of the public debt."[13] This statutory language does not specifically address the dividends paid on the preferred stock held by the Treasury, which are the subject of H.R. 678, discussed below.

Table 2. Incoming TARP Funds

($ in billions)

TARP Program	Asset Sales/Repayment of Loan Principal	Dividends and Interest	Capital Gains/Other Income	Warrant Proceeds	Total
Bank Support Programs	$230.23	$15.06	$9.38	$9.16	$263.83
Credit Market Programs	$3.70	$0.93	$0.08	$1.43	$44.43
AIG	$31.87	$0.64	$0.29	$0	$32.81
Auto Industry Financing Program	$35.18	$4.69	$0.73	$0	$40.60
Housing Support	Not applicable	Not applicable	Not applicable	Not applicable	Not applicable
Totals	$300.98	$21.32	$10.48	$9.16	$341.94

Source: May 15, 2012 Daily TARP Update.

Notes: Totals may not sum due to rounding. Housing support programs results in no assets to be sold, nor other income.

Table 3 summarizes TARP funds that have been disbursed but have not been repaid. Most of these funds are classified by the Treasury as "outstanding." This does not mean, however, that the

---

[12] See, for example, "7 Questions about the $700 Billion Bailout," *Time*, September 24, 2008, http://www.time.com/time/politics/article/0,8599,1843941,00.html and "Administration Is Seeking $700 Billion for Wall Street," *New York Times*, September 20, 2008, p. A1.

[13] P.L. 110-343, Section 106 (d).

recipient of these funds is obligated to repay these funds, as is typically the case with, for example, a loan that is outstanding from a bank to a borrower. Most of the outstanding TARP funds are embodied in assets, such as common stock, that recipients are not obligated to repay, instead, the Treasury is expected to sell these assets at a future date and hopefully recoup the funds that were disbursed. The TARP funds that are classified as a recognized loss, or as written off, are typically cases where either the asset sales were not sufficient to repay the initial TARP disbursement or a TARP recipient has failed, and thus is unable repay the funds.

Table 3. TARP Funds Outstanding or Lost

($ in billions)

TARP Program	Amount Outstanding	Recognized Loss/ Written Off
Bank Support Programs	$12.14	$2.75
Credit Market Programs	$14.73	$0
AIG	$30.44	$5.52
Auto Industry Financing Program	$37.14	$7.37
Housing Support	Not applicable	Not applicable
Totals	**$94.44**	**$15.64**

Source: May 15, 2012 Daily TARP Update.

Notes: Totals may not sum due to rounding. Housing support programs results in no assets to be sold, nor other income.

The Costs of TARP

In arriving at an overall cost to the government of TARP, or any similar program, it is important to account for the difference in time between initial outlay of funds and the receipt of any income. Some TARP contracts run for five years or more, and the difference in value between a dollar in 2008 and 2013, for example, could be significant. To compare dollar values over time, economists use present value calculations that reduce costs or income in the future relative to the present by a discount rate. Present value calculations can be very sensitive to the rate used if the amount of time involved is large. In preparing the budget cost estimates for TARP, the Administration and the Congressional Budget Office (CBO) are directed by Section 123 of EESA to adjust their estimates by current market borrowing rates, as opposed to the borrowing rate paid by Treasury. Using market rates instead of government borrowing rates increases the net calculated cost of these investments and is meant to better represent the true economic costs of the programs. The cost estimates for TARP have fallen dramatically since the program was started. For example, in March 2009, CBO estimated a $356 billion budgetary cost for TARP. This number fell to $109 billion in March 2010, and the latest CBO estimate is for a total budgetary cost of $32 billion.[14]

---

[14] Congressional Budget Office, *Director's Blog*, April 17, 2009, http://cbo.gov/publication/24884; *Report on the Troubled Asset Relief Program*, March 17, 2010, and March 28, 2012, http://cbo.gov/sites/default/files/cbofiles/ftpdocs/112xx/doc11227/03-17-tarp.pdf and http://cbo.gov/sites/default/files/cbofiles/attachments/03-28-2012TARP.pdf.

The various programs under TARP have very different estimated costs at the current time. In general, the bank support programs are estimated to produce a gain for the government and the credit market support programs are estimated to nearly break even. The losses in TARP are primarily estimated to accrue from the support for AIG, the automakers, and housing. **Table 4** summarizes recent detailed estimates of TARP's cost from CBO and the Administration. The largest difference between the Administration and CBO estimates are in the amounts expected to be disbursed for the housing support programs.

Table 4. Detailed Cost/Gain Estimates for TARP

($ in billions; gain(+)/loss(-))

TARP Program	OMB (Data from Nov. 2011)	CBO (Data from Feb. 2012)	Treasury (Data from Feb. 2012)
Capital Purchase Program	$6.7	$17	$14.7
Targeted Investment Program	$3.6	$8 (combined)	$4.0
Asset Guarantee Program	$3.6		$3.7
Community Development Capital Initiative	-$0.2	$0	$0.2
Term Asset-backed Lending Facility	-$0.4	$0	-$0.4
Public-Private Investment Program	$2.0	$0	$2.5
SBA 7(a) Securities	$0	$0	$0
AIG	-$24	-$22	-$17.6
Auto Industry Financing Program	-$24.8	-$19	-$21.7
Housing Support	-$45.6	-$16	-$45.6
Totals	**-$78.2**	**-32**	**-$59.8**

Sources: CBO, *Report on the Troubled Asset Relief Program—March 2012*; OMB, *Analytical Perspectives, FY2013 President's Budget*, Table 4-7; February 2012; April 2012 TARP 105(a) Report.

Notes: Totals may not sum due to rounding. CBO figures market "$0" are rounded from between -$500 million and +$500 million. AIG also received assistance through the Federal Reserve, which resulted in substantial asset holdings and income. These cost estimates do not include gains resulting from this assistance.

The cost estimates of TARP are sensitive to financial markets and the state of the economy. The ultimate cost of the program will depend largely on recouping value from the financial assets held in TARP. The assets resulting from bank support programs, including warrants and both preferred and common shares, have turned out to be relatively valuable, thus the estimates show an overall gain from these programs as the increases in asset values outweigh any losses from defaults. In the cases of AIG or the automakers, however, the estimates are that the assets held by the government through TARP ultimately will not return enough to recoup the TARP funds put into the companies.

The 112th Congress and TARP

The 112th Congress has shown a continued interest in TARP despite the expiration of the purchasing authority in October 2010. The first hearing of the House Committee on Oversight and Government Reform in the 112th Congress focused on TARP, with the Special Inspector

General for TARP and Treasury's Acting Assistant Secretary for Financial Stability as witnesses. Legislation that would affect TARP includes the following:

- **H.R. 189**, introduced on January 5, 2011, by Representative Rob Woodall, would repeal TARP in its entirety while allowing the Secretary to continue managing TARP assets to maximize future returns.

- **H.R. 430**, introduced on January 25, 2011, by Representative Jim Jordan, would terminate TARP's HAMP program and specifically return unobligated funds to the general fund.

- **H.R. 678**, introduced on February 11, 2011, by Representative Larry Kissell, would amend EESA to specifically include TARP dividend payments in the list of TARP proceeds that accrue to the general fund to pay down the national debt.

- **H.R. 830**, introduced on February 28, 2011, by Representative Robert Dold, would amend EESA to terminate the FHA Refinance Program. It passed the House on March 10, 2011, on a vote of 256-171.

- **H.R. 839**, introduced on February 28, 2011, by Representative Patrick McHenry, would terminate TARP's HAMP program. H.R. 839 was passed by the House on March 29, 2011, on a vote of 252-170.

- **H.R. 1315**, introduced on April 1, 2011, by Representative Sean Duffy, is focused on the Consumer Financial Protection Bureau. It was considered on the House floor under a rule, H.Res. 358, that added the text of H.R. 830 as Title II of H.R. 1315 prior to floor consideration. The amended bill passed the House on July 21, 2011. on a vote of 241-173.

- **H.R. 2434**, introduced on July 7, 2011, by Representative Jo Ann Emerson, would make appropriations for financial services and general government for FY2012 and included language to terminate HAMP.

- **H.R. 5652**, introduced on May 9, 2012, by Representative Paul Ryan, would provide for reconciliation pursuant to the concurrent resolution on the FY2013 budget and includes language to terminate HAMP.

- **S. 162**, introduced on January 25, 2011, by Senator Rand Paul, would repeal TARP in its entirety in addition to several other government programs.

- **S. 527**, introduced on March 9, 2011, by Senator Jim DeMint, would terminate TARP's HAMP program.

Ownership of Private Companies

Government ownership of common equity in private companies was not a general goal of EESA although it was expected that the government would be compensated for the assistance given to companies under TARP. In some cases, this compensation for TARP assistance has resulted in government holdings of common stock in amounts that typically would result in the government having a controlling interest in these companies. The government, however, has generally exercised little of the ownership control inherent in these large stakes. Common equity in companies has typically been accepted in return for TARP assistance in order to strengthen the companies' capital positions going forward. Such equity also provides a potential financial upside to the taxpayers if firms have a strong recovery, but has potential downside if firms do not recover strongly. Outstanding outlays, such as loans, that have been converted to common equity are no longer directly owed by the company to the government.

In the case of Citigroup, which converted $25 billion of preferred shares into common shares, the outcome for the government has been positive as the share price rose after the conversion, resulting in approximately $6.85 billion in capital gains for taxpayers. Ownership of Chrysler equity, however, turned out less positively for the government with the government realizing a $1.33 billion loss after the sale to Fiat. The outcome for GM and AIG remain uncertain. Both companies' stock prices would have to rise substantially from current levels to result in an overall gain from TARP. Sales of the common ownership stake in GMAC/Ally Financial have yet to begin.

Table 5 summarizes the current status of government ownership in large financial institutions.

Table 5. Companies with Large Government Common Ownership Stakes

($ in billions)

Company	Current Government Ownership Share	Total TARP Assistance Received[a]	Amount Recouped by the Treasury[b]	Losses Written Off or Realized	Total Outstanding Outlays[c]	Preferred Equity Outlays Outstanding[d]
AIG	61%[e]	$67.8	$32.8	$5.5	$30.4	$0
GM	32.0%	$50.2	$24.0	$4.4	$22.5	$0
GMAC/Ally Financial	73.8%	$17.2	$5.4	$0	$14.6	$5.9
Chrysler	0%	$10.9	$9.6	$2.9	$0	$0
Citigroup[f]	0%	$45 cash; $5 guarantee	$57.0	$0	$0	$0

Sources: March 15, 2012 TARP Daily Update, Various TARP 105(a) Reports, TARP Dividend and Interest Reports, and U.S. Treasury press releases.

a. Some of these companies received commitments for funds greater than the reported amounts, or other TARP assistance. These figures are actual dollars received by, or spent on behalf of, companies. In the case of GM and Chrysler, this includes before, during, and after their bankruptcies, and also includes amounts that went to support third party suppliers to GM and Chrysler.

b. Includes recoupment through bankruptcy proceeds, repayments, interest, dividends, and fees.

c. Includes outlays converted to common equity and thus not currently owed by the company to the government.

d. Does not include loans to bankrupt entities.

e. Federal Reserve loans that predate TARP resulted in 79.8% ownership of AIG. An additional 12.3% resulted from conversion of TARP preferred shares, including $1.6 billion in unpaid dividends. This conversion substantially diluted the initial 80% government stake. The government share has dropped from 92.1% due to equity sales.

f. $20 billion was repaid directly by Citigroup; $25 billion was converted into 34% of the equity in Citigroup, which was subsequently sold for $31.85 billion.

TARP and the Dodd-Frank Act[15]

Unlike EESA, which was a temporary response to the immediate financial crisis, the Dodd-Frank Wall Street Reform and Consumer Protection Act (the Dodd-Frank Act) was a broad bill that permanently changed many parts of the U.S. financial regulatory system. The act included a relatively short amendment to EESA in Title XIII, entitled the Pay It Back Act. Section 1302 of Dodd-Frank made three primary changes to EESA:

- reduced the overall authorization to purchase from nearly $700 billion[16] to $475 billion;

- removed the implicit authority for the Secretary to reuse TARP funds when TARP assets are sold;[17] and

- limited the authorities under the act to programs or initiatives initiated prior to June 25, 2010.

As of June 30, 2010, the Treasury reported that it planned to spend approximately $537 billion on the various programs, with $491 billion committed under signed contracts and $385 billion actually disbursed.[18] The July 21, 2010, enactment of the $475 billion limit in the Dodd-Frank Act thus required Treasury to reduce the amounts planned for TARP by more than $60 billion and the legal commitments under TARP by more than $16 billion. CBO scored the TARP changes in the Dodd-Frank Act as resulting in a decrease in direct spending of $11 billion in 2010.[19] The TARP changes reported by Treasury following the Dodd-Frank Act appear below in **Table 6**.

Under the broad authorities granted by EESA, Treasury could unilaterally change the planned program allocations. Following the Dodd-Frank Act, this authority was limited to the difference between the total of Treasury's plans and the total of the signed contracts, approximately $21 billion as of July 31, 2010.

---

[15] P.L. 111-203, see CRS Report R41350, *The Dodd-Frank Wall Street Reform and Consumer Protection Act: Issues and Summary*, coordinated by Baird Webel.

[16] The initial $700 billion had been reduced by $1.26 billion in P.L. 111-22.

[17] Section 115(a)(3) of EESA limits the Secretary's authority to purchase or guarantee assets to $700 billion "outstanding at any one time." While the interpretation was never subject to determination by the courts, this language can be read to allow total purchase of assets beyond $700 billion if assets are sold before additional purchases are made. Section 1302 of Dodd-Frank removed the phrase "outstanding at any one time."

[18] June 2010 TARP 105(a) Report.

[19] Congressional Budget Office, *CBO Estimate of the Net Deficit Effects of H.R. 4173, the Dodd-Frank Wall Street Reform and Consumer Protection Act*, June 29, 2010.

Table 6. TARP Changes Following the Dodd-Frank Act

($ in billions)

TARP Program	Planned Allocation Prior to Dodd-Frank	Change Following Dodd-Frank	Planned Allocation July 31, 2010	Legal Commitments July 31, 2010
Capital Purchase Program	$204.9	$0.0	$204.9	$204.9
Targeted Investment Program	$40.0	$0.0	$40.0	$40
Asset Guarantee Program	$5.0	$0.0	$5.0	$5.0
AIG (Systemically Significant Failing Institutions)	$69.8	$0.0	$69.8	$69.8
Term Asset-Backed Securities Program	$20.0	-$15.7	$4.3	$4.3
SBA Section 7(a)	$1.0	-$0.6	$0.4	
Community Development Capital Initiative	$0.8	$0.0	$0.8	$1.0[a]
Small Business Lending Fund	$30	-$30.0[b]	$0.0	$0.0
Public Private Investment Program	$30.4	-$7.9	$22.4	$22.4
Automotive Industry Financing Program	$84.8	-$3.1	$81.8	$81.8
Housing/HAMP	$48.7	-$3.1	$45.6	$30.25
Total	**$535.5**	**-60.5**	**$475.0**	**$454**

Source: July 2010 TARP 105(a) Report.

Notes: Figures may not add due to rounding.

a. Treasury's reporting did not separate the legal commitments for the two programs.

b. The Administration proposed creating a similar fund outside of TARP. See CRS Report R41385, *Small Business Legislation During the 111th Congress*, by Robert Jay Dilger and Gary Guenther.

Appendix. Details of TARP Programs

Bank Support Programs

Capital Purchase Program and Capital Assistance Program

Under the Capital Purchase Program (CPP), $125 billion in capital was immediately provided to the nine largest banks (which became eight after a merger), with up to another $125 billion reserved for smaller banks that might wish to apply for funds through their primary federal banking regulator. This capital was provided in the form of preferred share purchases by TARP under contracts between the Treasury and banks. The initial contracts with the largest banks (ultimately, eight rather than nine) prevented these banks from exiting the program for three years. The contracts included dividend payments to be made on the preferred shares outstanding and the granting of warrants to the government. By the end of 2008, the CPP had 214 participating banks with approximately $172.5 billion in share purchases outstanding.

The Obama Administration and the 111th Congress implemented changes to the CPP. EESA was amended, placing additional restrictions on participating banks in the existing CPP contracts, but also allowing for early repayment and withdrawal from the program without financial penalty.[20] With the advent of more stringent executive compensation restrictions for TARP recipients, many banks began to repay, or attempt to repay, TARP funds. According to Treasury reports, by June 30, 2009, $70.1 billion of $203.2 billion CPP funds had been repaid; by December 31, 2009, $121.9 billion of $204.9 billion had been repaid; and by December 31, 2010, $167.93 billion of $204.9 billion had been repaid.

The new Administration also announced a review of the banking system, in which the largest participants were subject to stress tests to assess the adequacy of their capital levels. Satisfactory performance in the stress test was one regulatory requirement for large firms that wished to repay TARP funds. Large firms that appear too fragile in the stress test would be required to raise additional capital, and the firms would have the option of raising that capital privately or from the government through a new Capital Assistance Program. No funding was provided through the Capital Assistance Program, although GMAC, formerly General Motors' financing arm, received funding to meet stress test requirements through the Automotive Industry Financing Program (discussed below). In addition, Citigroup, one of the initial eight large banks receiving TARP funds, agreed with the government to convert its TARP preferred shares into common equity to meet stress test requirements (see discussion of Citigroup below).

CPP profits stem from dividend payments and warrants received from recipients, and capital gains in limited cases when shares are sold for more than face value (the standard CPP shares are resold at face value). Losses stem from failure to repay in part or full. The ultimate profitability of the program will be determined by the balance between the two.

Realized losses to date on the CPP preferred shares have been relatively small. As of May 2012, Treasury reported $2.58 billion in write-offs and $0.17 billion in realized losses from the CPP.

---

[20] Title VII of the American Recovery and Reinvestment Act of 2009 (P.L. 111-5,123 Stat. 115).

The majority of this amount was due to the failure of CIT Group, which had $2.3 billion in TARP shares outstanding when it failed.

An indication of how many preferred shares may currently be at risk of future losses might be gleaned from the number of recipients who have missed dividend or interest payments. At the end of April 2012, 237 CPP recipients had missed at least one payment with a total of $305.7 million in missed dividend and interest payments, approximately 2.6% of the $11.6 billion in such payments that had been received.[21] This may be a misleading measure of troubled participants, however, because there is no financial penalty for missing a dividend payment. Missed dividend payments are simply rolled into the outstanding balance, although multiple missed dividend payments do give Treasury the right to appoint members to the board of the institution. Thus, healthy banks could be missing dividend payments to increase the amount of capital available to support their business. In practice, two studies have claimed that dividend skippers tend to be weaker institutions.[22] Alternatively, some of the banks who cannot afford dividend payments now may become more profitable as the economy recovers and ultimately repay TARP funds.

Another source of CPP profits are the proceeds from the warrants received from the companies. Treasury has not generally exercised warrants to take common stock in CPP recipients. Following the contracts initially agreed upon, Treasury has allowed institutions to purchase their warrants directly upon repayment of preferred shares, as long as both sides can reach an acceptable price. To reach an initial offering price, Treasury is using complex option pricing models to price the warrants that require assumptions to be made about future prices and interest rates. Since these pricing models are by their nature uncertain, some critics urge Treasury to auction the warrants on the open market (allowing the issuing firm to bid as well) to ensure that Treasury receives a fair price for them. Open auctions have been used, but only when an agreement between the Treasury and the firms cannot be reached.

CPP also earns income from dividends with a rate of 5% for the first five years, and 9% thereafter. (For S-Corp banks, the dividend rate is 7.7% for the first five years and 13.8% thereafter.)

Table A-1 below summarizes the CPP, including current and peak asset holdings, losses or gains, and conditions of the program.

---

[21] April 2012 TARP Dividends and Interest Report.

[22] Dobrina Georgieva, Linus Wilson "TARP's Dividend Skippers," Working Paper, Social Science Research Network, August 6, 2010; Linus Wilson "TARP's Deadbeat Banks," Working Paper, Social Science Research Network, August 15, 2010.

Table A-1. Capital Purchase Program

Federal Government				Terms and Conditions		
Latest Asset Holdings	Asset Holdings at Peak	Total Income	Expected Gains(+)/ Losses(-)	Dividend Rate	Warrants	Expiration Date
$11.56 billion	$198.8 billion (Mar 30, 2009)	$26.11 billion (less $2.75 billion in losses)	+$15 billion (Treasury); +$17 billion (CBO)	5% for first 5 years, 9% thereafter[a]	15% of preferred shares (5% immediately exercised for privately- held banks)	Preferred Shares outstanding until repaid. No new contracts/modifications after Oct. 3, 2010.

Source: May 15, 2012 Daily TARP Update; May 2012 TARP 105(a) Report; CBO, *Report on the Troubled Asset Relief Program—March 2012*; Various TARP Transactions Reports.

Notes: Data includes preferred shares to Citigroup and Bank of America under CPP, which are also detailed in sections on assistance to those companies below.

a.   For S-Corp banks, the dividend rate is 7.7% for the first five years and 13.8% thereafter.

Community Development Capital Initiative

The Community Development Capital Initiative (CDCI) operated somewhat like the CPP in that it purchased preferred shares from financial institutions, and in some cases institutions were permitted to convert previous CPP preferred shares to CDCI preferred shares. The program was specifically focused on institutions that serve low-income, underserved communities. Treasury purchased preferred shares from institutions that qualified for the CDCI up to an amount equal to 5% of the institutions' risk-weighted assets for banks and thrifts or 3.5% of total assets for credit unions. These preferred shares pay an initial dividend rate of 2%, which will increase to 9% after eight years. Unlike the CPP, no warrants in the financial institutions were included. Purchases under the program were completed in September of 2010 with approximately $210 million new shares purchased. In addition, approximately $360 million of shares were converted from CPP shares.

Table A-2. Community Development Capital Initiative

Federal Government				Terms and Conditions		
TARP Funds Outstanding	Funds Disbursed at Peak	TARP Income	Current or Expected Gains(+)/ Losses(-)	Interest/ Dividend Rate	Warrants	Expiration Date
$570 million	$570 million	$20 million	-$170 million (Treasury)	2% (9% after 8 years)	none	No new purchases after Oct. 2010.

Source: March 15 2012 TARP Daily Update; April 2012 TARP 105(a) Report.

Note: Of the disbursed funds, $210 million are new shares and $360 million are shares transferred from CPP.

Targeted Investment Program and Asset Guarantee Program

The Targeted Investment Program (TIP) and the Asset Guarantee Program (AGP) were only used as part of a package to aid two large banks, Citigroup and Bank of America, which were also large recipients of CPP funds. The combined assistance for these banks are addressed below, rather than treat the TIP and AGP as separate programs.

Citigroup (CPP/TIP/AGP)

On November, 23, 2008, the Treasury, Federal Reserve, and FDIC announced a joint intervention in Citigroup, which had previously been a recipient of $25 billion in TARP Capital Purchase Program funding, to "[support] financial stability."[23] This exceptional intervention consisted of an additional $20 billion purchase of preferred shares through the TARP Targeted Investment Program and a government guarantee for a pool of $306 billion in Citigroup assets (reduced to $301 billion when the guarantee was finalized on January 16, 2009) through the TARP Asset Guarantee Program, FDIC, and Federal Reserve. Citigroup paid the federal government a fee for the guarantee in the form of $4 billion in trust preferred securities paying an 8% dividend rate. The Treasury also received warrants in both of these transactions.

On February 27, 2009, Citigroup and Treasury officials agreed that the Treasury Department would convert $25 billion of its TARP CPP investment in Citigroup preferred stock into Citigroup common stock and cancel the warrants taken by Treasury under the CPP. After this conversion, the U.S. government owned approximately 33.6% (7.7 million shares) of Citigroup common stock. The conversion of preferred shares to common stock worsened the government's priority on Citigroup's assets in the event of liquidation, but improved certain capital ratios for the company and relieved it of the obligation to pay dividends to the government, as it had previously with the preferred shares. The conversion exposed the government to more potential risk as well as to potential upside reward. The government's preferred shares could only be redeemed at par value, regardless of the performance of the company, while the government's holdings of common stock rose and fell in value based on the market valuation of the company.

In December 2009, Citigroup and the Treasury reached an agreement to repay the outstanding $20 billion in preferred securities and to cancel the asset guarantee. As part of this agreement, Treasury agreed to cancel $1.8 billion worth of the $4 billion in trust preferred securities originally paid as a fee for the guarantee. Citigroup repurchased the outstanding AGP trust preferred securities on September 30, 2009. While the asset guarantee was in place, no losses were claimed and no federal funds were paid out. Warrants received under the TIP and AGP, with a strike price of $10.61, are still held by the Treasury.

In April 2010, the Treasury began selling its common share holdings in Citigroup. The shares were sold in tranches through 2010, with a total of 4.1 million shares being sold by the end of September 2010. Treasury announced the completion of the sales early in December 2010. The average sales price for the Treasury shares was $4.14 per share compared with an initial conversion price of $3.25 per share. The gain from the common stock sales was approximately $6.9 billion, along with approximately $2.2 billion from the sales of the remaining trust preferred securities granted as a fee from the AGP, $2.9 billion in interest and dividends, and $54 million

---

[23] U.S. Treasury, "Joint Statement by Treasury, Federal Reserve, and FDIC on Citigroup," press release hp-1287, November 23, 2008.

from the sale of warrants for a total nominal gain (i.e., not discounted for market risk) from the Citigroup intervention of $12.1 billion.[24]

Table A-3 below summarizes the assistance for Citigroup through the CPP, TIP, and AGP, including current and peak asset holdings, losses or gains, and conditions of the program.

Table A-3. Citigroup Support (CPP/TIP/AGP)

	Federal Government				Terms and Conditions			
Program	Current Asset Holdings/ Guarantees	Asset Holdings/ Guarantees at Peak	Total Income	Realized Capital Gains(+)/ Losses(-)	Dividend/Fee	Warrants Issued	Subsequent Conversion/ Amendment	Expiration Date
Capital Purchase Program	$0	$25 billion	$0.9 billion (dividends); $.05 billion (warrants)	+$6.9 billion	preferred: 5% dividend for first 5 years, 9% thereafter; common: none	210 million with a strike price of $17.85 per share	Converted preferred shares to common stock, subsequently sold for $31.9 billion.	None, shares outstanding until sold or repurchased.
Targeted Investment Program	$0	$20 billion trust preferred securities (until Dec. 2009)	$1.6 billion (dividends); $0.19 billion (warrants)	$0	8% dividend	188,5 million with a strike price of $10.61	Converted preferred shares to trust preferred securities.	None, shares or securities outstanding until sold or repurchased.
Asset Guarantee Program	$0	$301 billion (up to $244.8 billion of losses borne by Fed, Treasury and FDIC) (until Dec. 2009)	$0.44 billion (dividends); $0.07 billion (warrants); $50 million termination fee to Fed	$2.2 billion	following termination, $2.2 billion in trust preferred securities with 8% dividend	66,5 million with a strike price of $10.61 per share	$1.8 billion canceled upon termination of Asset Guarantee.	Nov. 2018 (residential assets)/Nov. 2013 (non-residential assets)

Sources: May 15 2012 Daily TARP Update; October 2011 TARP 105(a) Report; October 2011 TARP Dividends and Interest Report; SIGTARP, *Extraordinary Financial Assistance Provided to Citigroup, Inc*, January 13, 2011; U.S. Treasury press release, December 10, 2010.

Note: Assistance to Citigroup through CPP is also included in the CPP Table.

Bank of America (CPP/TIP/AGP)

On January 16, 2009, the Treasury, the Federal Reserve, and the FDIC announced a joint intervention in Bank of America, which had previously been a recipient of $25 billion in TARP Capital Purchase Program funds,[25] "as part of its commitment to support financial market

---

[24] U.S. Treasury, "Taxpayers Receive $10.5 Billion in Proceeds Today From Final Sale of Treasury Department Citigroup Common Stock," press release, December 10, 2010, http://www.financialstability.gov/latest/ pr_12102010 html, and TARP Transactions Report, January 26, 2011.

[25] As part of this transaction, the government received warrants for 121,792,790 shares with a strike price of $30.79.

---

stability."[26] This exceptional assistance included the purchase of an additional $20 billion of Bank of America preferred shares through the TARP Targeted Investment Program[27] and a joint guarantee on a pool of up to $118 billion of Bank of America's assets (largely acquired through its merger with Merrill Lynch) through the TARP Asset Guarantee Program, the FDIC, and the Federal Reserve. Bank of America was to pay the federal government a fee for the guarantee in the form of $4 billion in preferred stock with an 8% dividend rate and warrants to purchase common stock worth $2.4 billion at the time of the agreement.

While the asset guarantee was announced in January 2009, a final agreement was never signed. On September 21, 2009, Bank of America announced that it had negotiated a $425 million termination fee that allowed it to withdraw from the AGP, canceling the warrants and preferred shares issued for the program.

On December 9, 2009, Treasury announced that Bank of America had repurchased the $45 billion in preferred stock previously purchased under TARP. The warrants issued under the CPP and the TIP were sold at auction by the government in March 2010 for approximately $1.6 billion. No government assistance to Bank of America remains outstanding.

Table A-4 below summarizes the support for Bank of America through the CPP, TIP, and AGP, including current and peak asset holdings, losses or gains, and conditions of the support.

Table A-4. Bank of America Support (CPP/TIP/AGP)

	Federal Government				Terms and Conditions		
Program	Current Asset Holdings/ Guarantees	Asset Holdings/ Guarantees at Peak	Total Income	Realized Capital Gains(+)/ Losses(-)	Dividend Rate/Fee	Warrants	Expiration Date
Capital Purchase Program	$0	$25 billion (until Dec. 2009)[a]	$1.3 billion (dividends); $0.3 billion (warrants)	$0	5% for first 5 years, 9% thereafter	121,792,790 warrants sold for $0.3 billion.	None, shares outstanding until repurchased.
Targeted Investment Program	$0	$20 billion (until Dec. 2009)	$1.4 billion (dividends): $1.25 billion (warrants)	$0	8%	150,375,940 warrants sold for $1.25 billion	None, shares outstanding until repurchased.
Asset Guarantee Program	$0	$118 billion (up to $97.2 billion of losses borne by Fed, Treasury and FDIC) (never finalized)	$425 million termination fee to government ($57 million termination fee to Fed)	n/a	n/a	n/a	Jan. 2019 (residential assets)/Jan. 2014 (non-residential assets).

---

[26] U.S. Treasury, "Treasury, Federal Reserve, and the FDIC Provide Assistance to Bank of America," press release hp1356, January 16, 2009.

[27] As part of this transaction, the government received warrants for 150,375,940 shares with a strike price of $13.30.

Source: May 15 2012 Daily TARP Update; October 2011 TARP 105(a) Report; October 2011 TARP Dividends and Interest Report; Congressional Budget Office, *Budget and Economic Outlook,* January 2010; SIGTARP, *Quarterly Report to Congress,* January 30, 2010; OMB, *Analytical Perspectives, FY2011 President's Budget,* Table 4-7; February 2010.

Notes: Assistance to Bank of America through CPP is also included in the CPP Table.

a. Of the $25 billion of preferred shares, $10 billion were originally issued by Merrill Lynch, which subsequently merged with Bank of America.

Credit Market Programs

Public Private Investment Program

On March 23, 2009, Treasury announced the Public Private Investment Program (PPIP). PPIP as envisioned consisted of two asset purchase programs designed to leverage private funds with government funds to remove troubled assets from bank balance sheets. Perhaps closer to the original conception of TARP than other TARP programs, PPIP dedicated TARP resources as equity to (1) acquire troubled loans in a fund partially guaranteed by the FDIC and (2) acquire troubled securities in a fund designed to be used with loans from the Federal Reserve's TALF program or TARP. Both funds would match TARP money with private investment, and profits or losses would be shared between the government and the private investors. Unlike the original conception of TARP, private investors would choose the assets to purchase and manage the funds and the day-to-day disposition of assets. Treasury originally envisioned assets purchases through PPIP would be as high as $1 trillion (using as much as $200 billion in TARP funds), but ultimately Treasury reports only $21.86 billion of TARP funds obligated to the program with $17.96 billion disbursed as of May 15, 2012.

Legacy Loan Program

A legacy loan is a problem loan that is already on a bank's balance sheet, as opposed to a potential new loan or refinance. The Legacy Loan Program was intended to reduce uncertainty about bank balance sheets and draw private capital to the financial services sector by providing FDIC debt guarantees and Treasury equity co-investment to fund private-public entities purchasing problem loans from banks. The program, however, was not implemented beyond a single pilot legacy loan sale reported by the FDIC on September 30, 2009. In this pilot sale, the FDIC auctioned a portfolio of residential mortgages with unpaid principal of $1.3 billion from a bank that the FDIC had taken into receivership. Residential Credit Solutions placed a winning bid of $64 million to receive a 50% stake in this pool, and financed the purchase with $728 million of debt guaranteed by the FDIC.[28]

Legacy Securities Program

The larger part of the PPIP is designed to deal with existing mortgage-related securities on bank balance sheets. There are several basic steps to the Legacy Securities Program (S-PPIP). Investors

---

[28] Federal Deposit Insurance Corporation, "Legacy Loans Program – Winning Bidder Announced in Pilot Sale," press release, September 16, 2009, http://www.fdic.gov/news/news/press/2009/pr09172 html. FDIC reports seven other public-private partnership transactions since 2008, but classifies only the September 2009 transaction as a PPIP transaction.

identify non-agency MBS that were originally rated AAA. Agency MBS refer to loans issued by GSEs, such as Fannie Mae and Freddie Mac, and non-agency MBS refers to mortgage-related securities issued by private financial institutions, such as investment banks. Private fund managers apply to Treasury to pre-qualify to raise funds to participate in the program. Approved fund managers that raise private equity capital receive matching Treasury capital and an additional loan to the fund that matches the private capital (thus far, the private investor that raises $100 has a total of $300 available). In addition to this basic transaction, Treasury reserves discretion to allow up to another matching loan so that, in some cases, raising $100 makes a total of $400 available.

Nine funds were pre-qualified by the Treasury in June 2009. In early January 2010, however, one of the funds reached a liquidation agreement with Treasury and was wound down.[29] As of September 30, 2010, PPIP funds had raised $7.4 billion of private equity capital, to be matched by $22.1 billion in TARP equity and debt capital.[30]

Table A-5. Public Private Investment Program

	Federal Government				Terms and Conditions		
Program	Funds Disbursed/ Guaranteed	Funds Disbursed/ Guaranteed at Peak	Total Income	Current or Expected Gains(+)/ Losses(-)[a]	Interest/ Dividend Rate	Warrants	Expiration Date
Legacy Securities	$16.3 billion	$16.3 billion	$1.2 billion	$0 billion (CBO); $2.5 billion (Treasury)	LIBOR plus "applicable margin"	yes (amount unspecified)	10 years from creation of fund.
Legacy Loans	$728 million	$728 million	n/a		no contracts	yes (amount unspecified)	No new contracts/ modifications after Oct. 3, 2010.

Sources: May 15 2012 Daily TARP Update; April 2012 TARP 105(a) Report; U.S. Treasury, *Legacy Securities Public-Private Investment Program Update*, April 19, 2012; Congressional Oversight Panel September 2009 Oversight Report; SIGTARP, *Quarterly Report to Congress*, January 30, 2010; CBO, *Report on the Troubled Asset Relief Program—March 2012*; Data on Structured Loan Sales from FDIC.

Note: For legacy securities, funds disbursed to date (not committed). For legacy loans, loans guaranteed.

a. Expected losses for Legacy Securities and Legacy Loans combined.

Term Asset-Backed Securities Loan Facility

The Term Asset-Backed Securities Loan Facility (TALF) is a Fed program to assist the asset-backed security market, with TARP acting as a backstop in case of any losses. TALF income

---

[29] December 2009 TARP 105(a) Report, pp. 15, 30-32.

[30] U.S. Treasury, *Legacy Securities Public-Private Investment Program Update*, April 19, 2012, p. 3, available at http://www.treasury.gov/initiatives/financial-stability/programs/Credit%20Market%20Programs/ppip/Documents/PPIP%20Report%20-%20Q1-12.pdf.

accrues to the Fed with possible losses and some expenses accruing to the Treasury. As of May 15, 2012, Treasury reported $0.1 billion in disbursements for TALF.[31]

Table A-6. Term Asset-Backed Securities Loan Facility

	Federal Government				Terms and Conditions		
Program	Funds Disbursed/ Guaranteed	Funds Disbursed/ Guaranteed at Peak	Total Income	Current or Expected Gains(+)/ Losses(-)[a]	Interest/ Dividend Rate	Warrants	Expiration Date
TALF	$100 million	$100 million	$0	$430 million (Treasury)	n/a	none	No new purchases after June 30, 2010.

Sources: May 15 2012 Daily TARP Update; April 2012 TARP 105(a) Report; Federal Reserve Bank of New York.

Section 7(a) Securities Purchase Program

This program supports the Small Business Administration's (SBA) Section 7(a) loan program through purchasing pooled SBA guaranteed securities backed by private loans to small businesses.[32] Beginning in March 2010, Treasury purchased a total of $368 million in securities guaranteed by the SBA. Purchases ended in October 2010 with the expiration of the TARP authority.

Table A-7. Public Private Investment Program

	Federal Government				Terms and Conditions		
Program	Funds Disbursed/ Guaranteed	Funds Disbursed/ Guaranteed at Peak	Total Income	Current or Expected Gains(+)/ Losses(-)[a]	Interest/ Dividend Rate	Warrants	Expiration Date
Section 7(a) Securities	$0	$368 million	$9 million	$0 (Treasury)	floating	none	No new purchases after Oct. 2010.

Sources: May 15 2012 Daily TARP Update; April 2012 TARP 105(a) Report; SIG TARP Quarterly Report to Congress, April 25, 2012.

---

[31] For additional information on TALF, see CRS Report RL34427, *Financial Turmoil: Federal Reserve Policy Responses*, by Marc Labonte.

[32] For additional information on this program, see CRS Report R41146, *Small Business Administration 7(a) Loan Guaranty Program*, by Robert Jay Dilger.

U.S. Automaker Assistance[33]

In addition to financial firms, non-financial firms have also sought support under TARP, most notably U.S. automobile manufacturers.[34] While EESA specifically authorized the Secretary of the Treasury to purchase troubled assets from "financial firms," the legislative definition of this term did not mention manufacturing companies.[35] After specific legislation for the automakers failed to clear Congress,[36] the Bush Administration turned to TARP for funding.

On December 19, 2008, the Bush Administration announced it was providing support through TARP to General Motors and Chrysler under the Automotive Industry Financing Program (AIFP). The initial package included up to $13.4 billion in a secured loan to GM and $4 billion in a secured loan to Chrysler. In addition, $884 million was lent to GM for its participation in a rights offering by GMAC as GM's former financing arm was becoming a bank holding company. On December 29, 2008, the Treasury announced that GMAC also was to receive a $5 billion capital injection through preferred share purchases.

After January 21, 2009, the Obama Administration continued assistance for the automakers, including support for the automaker warranties under the AIFP (so that consumers would not be discouraged from purchasing cars during the restructuring), and for third-party suppliers to the automakers (the Automotive Supplier Support Program, ASSP). Additional loans for GM and Chrysler were made before and during the two companies' bankruptcies, and GMAC received additional capital through preferred share purchases as well. At the end of 2009, GM had received approximately $49.5 billion in direct loans; Chrysler had outstanding commitments for $12.9 billion in loans and drawn approximately $10.9 billion; GMAC had received $17.2 billion in preferred equity purchases; and Chrysler Financial had received $1.5 billion in loans. Some of this assistance is still owed by the companies, some has been repaid, and some has been converted into common equity in the company receiving assistance.

As of May 15, 2012, TARP support for the auto industry totaled approximately $79.7 billion disbursed, with $35.18 billion repaid and $5.42 billion in income. Approximately $7.4 billion has been written off or taken as a realized loss and $37.14 billion of assistance is outstanding. The assistance outstanding takes the form of (1) government ownership of 32.04% of post-bankruptcy GM; and (2) government ownership of 73.8% government ownership of GMAC (which has changed its name to Ally Financial), with $5.9 billion in preferred equity outstanding. In addition, $849 million in loans to Old (pre-bankruptcy) GM and $1.8 billion in loans to Old (pre-

---

[33] This section was prepared with the assistance of Bill Canis, CRS specialist in Industrial Organization and Business. For a comprehensive analysis of federal financial assistance to U.S. automakers, see CRS Report R40003, *U.S. Motor Vehicle Industry: Federal Financial Assistance and Restructuring*, coordinated by Bill Canis. Statistics in the section are taken from the December TARP 105(a) Report, from Congressional Oversight Panel, *September Oversight Report: The Use of TARP Funds in the Support and Reorganization of the Domestic Automotive Industry*, September 9, 2009, available at http://cop.senate.gov/documents/cop-090909-report.pdf and from various contracts posted by the U.S. Treasury at http://www.treasury.gov/initiatives/financial-stability/investment-programs/aifp/Pages/autoprogram.aspx.

[34] See, for example, Statement by Secretary of the Treasury Henry Paulson in U.S. Congress, House Committee on Financial Services, *Oversight of Implementation of the Emergency Economic Stabilization Act of 2008 and of Government Lending and Insurance Facilities: Impact on the Economy and Credit Availability*, 110th Cong., 2nd sess., November 18, 2008.

[35] P.L. 110-343, Division A, Section 3.

[36] In December 2008, the House of Representatives passed H.R. 7321, authorizing the use of certain Department of Energy funds as bridge loans to GM and Chrysler. Passed by a vote of 237-170, the bill was not acted upon in the Senate.

---

bankruptcy) Chrysler have not been repaid and neither amount appears likely to be repaid. The loan to Chrysler Financial was completely repaid with interest.

For the outstanding assistance, the extent to which the government recoups its TARP funds will depend substantially on how much is eventually received when the government sells its equity interests. The government has already sold a portion of its stake in New GM at a price of $33 per share. The remaining shares would have to reach approximately $54 for the government to be able to recoup the nominal value of its $50.2 billion assistance for the company.[37] Treasury estimates of assistance to the auto industry made with February 2012 data are for a lifetime cost of $21.7 billion, whereas CBO estimated the subsidy cost to be $19 billion in March 2012.

Table A-8 below summarizes the support for the automakers, including current and peak asset holdings or loan amounts, losses or gains, and conditions of the assistance.

Table A-8. Government Support for the Auto Industry

Beneficiary/ Program	Federal Government				Terms and Conditions		
	Latest Balance Owed	Total Assistance at Peak	Total Income	Current or Expected Gain(+)/ Loss(-)	Dividend/ Interest Rate	Subsequent Conversion	Expiration Date
General Motors	$0 (new GM); $849 million (old GM); $22.5 billion outstanding, but not owed by GM.	$50.2 billion combined loans (not including $884 million loan for GMAC rights offering)	$0.86 billion	-$4.4 billion (actual capital loss due to stock sale)	LIBOR + 5%	Loan converted into 60.8 % of common equity and preferred stock; 27.5% of common equity sold for $13.5 billion.	January 2015 (new GM loan); December 2011 (old GM loan)
GMAC/Ally Financial	$5.9 billion preferred equity; $8.7 billion outstanding but not owed by Ally.	$17.2 billion preferred equity and $884 million loan through GM.	$2.86 billion	Not Reported	9%	Loan and preferred shares converted into 73.8% of common equity	No expiration
Chrysler	$0	$10.9 billion loan; ($2.1 billion never drawn)	$1.6 billion	-$2.9 billion (actual loss)	LIBOR + 7.9% ; LIBOR + 3%; LIBOR + 5%	9.9% of common equity; subsequently reduced to 8.6%	June 2017 (new Chrysler loan); January 2012 (old Chrysler loan)
Chrysler Financial	$0	$1.5 billion loan	$7 million	n/a		None	January 2014

---

[37] See CRS Report R41978, *The Role of TARP Assistance in the Restructuring of General Motors*, by Bill Canis and Baird Webel.

Sources: May 15, 2012 Daily TARP Update; April 2012 TARP 105(a) Report; March 2012 TARP Dividends and Interest Report; Congressional Oversight Panel, *September 2009 Oversight Report;* CBO, *Report on the Troubled Asset Relief Program—March 2012;* SIGTARP, *Quarterly Report to Congress,* September 30, 2010.

Note: LIBOR = London Interbank Offered Rate.

American International Group

In the fall of 2008, American International Group (AIG) was a federally chartered thrift holding company regulated by the Office of Thrift Supervision (OTS) at the holding company level, with a broad range of businesses, primarily insurance subsidiaries, which are state-chartered and state-regulated.[38] Facing losses on various operations, AIG experienced a significant decline in its stock price and downgrades from the major credit rating agencies. These downgrades led to immediate demands for significant amounts of collateral (approximately $14 billion to $15 billion in collateral payments, according to contemporary press reports).[39] As financial demands on the company mounted, bankruptcy appeared a possibility, as had occurred with Lehman Brothers on September 15, 2008. Many feared that AIG was "too big to fail" due to the potential for widespread disruption to financial markets resulting from such a failure.

On September 16, 2008 (prior to the existence of TARP), the Fed announced that it was taking action to support AIG in the form of a secured two-year line of credit with a value of up to $85 billion and a high interest rate. In addition, the government received warrants to purchase up to 79.9% of the equity in AIG. On October 8, 2008, the Fed announced that it would lend AIG up to an additional $37.8 billion against securities held by its insurance subsidiaries. In October 2008, AIG also announced that it had applied to the Fed's general Commercial Paper Funding Facility (CPFF) and was approved to borrow up to $20.9 billion at the facility's standard terms.

In early November 2008 (following the creation of TARP), the financial support for AIG was restructured. The restructured financial support consisted of (1) reducing the size of the Fed loan to up to $60 billion, with the term lengthened to five years and the interest rate reduced by 5.5%; (2) purchasing of $40 billion in preferred shares through TARP; and (3) replacing the $37.8 billion loan, with up to $52.5 billion total in asset purchases by the Fed through two Limited Liability Corporations (LLCs) known as Maiden Lane II and Maiden Lane III. The 79.9% equity position of the government in AIG remained essentially unchanged after the restructuring of the intervention.

In March 2009, the assistance was restructured further through (1) a partial payback of the Fed loan through a swap of debt for equity in two AIG subsidiaries worth approximately $25 billion, reducing the maximum to $35 billion; and (2) commitments for additional future TARP purchases of up to $29.8 billion in preferred shares at AIG's discretion, and the conversion of existing shares into shares with optional dividend payments.[40] The Maiden Lane LLCs continued operating under

---

[38] For a comprehensive analysis of federal assistance to AIG, see CRS Report R40438, *Federal Government Assistance for American International Group (AIG),* by Baird Webel.

[39] See, for example, "U.S. to Take Over AIG in $85 Billion Bailout; Central Banks Inject Cash as Credit Dries Up," *Wall Street Journal,* September 17, 2008, pp. A1-A6.

[40] AIG issued $1.6 billion of additional preferred shares to the government in recognition of accrued, unpaid dividends on the initial $40 billion in assistance. AIG has not paid dividends since the conversion to optional dividends, with a total of $6.7 billion in missed dividend payments as of September 30, 2010, according to the Special Inspector General for TARP, http://www.sigtarp.gov/reports/congress/2010/October2010_Quarterly_Report_to_Congress.pdf. These missed payments gave Treasury the right to appoint two directors to AIG's board.

the previous terms, with the actual loans extended to the LLCs totaling $43.9 billion at their peak of the possible $52.5 billion. AIG's access to the CPFF had been reduced to $15.9 billion in January 2009, due to a ratings agency downgrade. AIG continued to access this facility until it expired in February 2010.

In September 2010, AIG and the government announced another restructuring of the government's assistance. This restructuring closed on January 14, 2011. The expressed goal was to simplify the government's interest in AIG and provide for a path for the divestment of the government's stake in AIG. The essence of the plan called for (1) ending the Fed's involvement with AIG through loan repayment and transfer of the Fed's equity interests to the Treasury and (2) converting the government's $49.1 billion in existing preferred shares into common shares, which can then be sold to the public over time. The specific steps involved several interlocking transactions, including the initial public offering (IPO) of a large AIG subsidiary, the sale of several other AIG subsidiaries, and the use of up to approximately $20 billion in TARP funds to transfer equity interests from the Fed to the Treasury. Once these transactions closed, the Treasury held 92% of AIG's common equity (1.66 billion shares) and equity interests in AIG's subsidiaries worth approximately $20.3 billion.

Since January 2011, successive sales of both AIG common equity and the AIG subsidiary equity has reduced the outstanding assistance to AIG. The current government interests resulting from the AIG assistance include the following:

- Approximately 61% (1.06 billion shares) of AIG's common equity are held by the Treasury.

- The Fed continues to hold an interest in the Maiden Lane III LLC created in November 2008. As of May 10, 2012, the Fed reports $8.7 billion in loans and accrued interest are outstanding with sufficient equity holdings to provide an additional $4 billion in capital gains.

The government's ability to recoup its funds from the AIG rescue will depend mainly on how much it eventually receives when it sells its equity interests. The **Table A-2** below summarizes the support received by AIG from both TARP and the Fed, including current and peak asset holdings, losses or gains, and conditions of the support.

Table A-9. AIG Support

	Federal Government				Terms and Conditions			
Program	Outstanding Amount	Outstanding Amount at Peak	Total Income	Current or Expected Gain(+) /Loss(-)	Dividend/ Interest Rate	Warrants/ Equity Interests	Subsequent Conversion	Expiration Date
TARP Systemically Significant Failing Institutions	$30.44 billion	$67.84 billion	$0.93 billion in dividends paid and capital gains.	-$22 billion (CBO); -$17.6 billion (Treasury)	10% (dividends paid at AIG's discretion)	warrants for 2% of common shares	$49.1 billion[a] converted to AIG common equity; $20.3 billion converted subsidiary equity	Mar. 2014

	Federal Government				Terms and Conditions			
Program	Outstanding Amount	Outstanding Amount at Peak	Total Income	Current or Expected Gain(+) /Loss(-)	Dividend/ Interest Rate	Warrants/ Equity Interests	Subsequent Conversion	Expiration Date
Fed Loan to AIG	$0	$87.3 billion loan (Oct. 2008)	$8.2 billion in interest and dividends	$16.4 billion from equity holdings (Treasury)	3 month LIBOR+3%	warrants for 79.9% (later reduced to 77.9%) of common shares	Reduced balance by $25 billion in exchange for equity in life insurance subsidiaries	Sept. 2013
Fed Loan for Troubled Asset Purchases	$8.0 billion in loans to purchase assets	$43.9 billion loans to purchase assets (Dec. 2008)	$2.9 billion (plus $0.7 billion unpaid accrued interest)	$0 ($4 billion unrealized capital gain)	LIBOR+1%	none	n/a	None; securities held until sold or until maturity.
Fed Commercial Paper Funding Facility	$0	$16.2 billion (Jan. 2009)	Not reported	n/a	overnight index swap (OIS) rate+1%; OIS+3%	none	n/a	Feb. 2010

Sources: May 15 2012 TARP Daily Update; April 2012 TARP 105(a) Report; Federal Reserve, statistical release H.4.1, *Factors Affecting Reserve Balances of Depository Institutions and Condition Statement of Federal Reserve Banks*, November 25, 2011; Federal Reserve Bank of New York, "Actions Related to AIG," http://www.newyorkfed.org/aboutthefed/aig/index.html; CBO, *Report on the Troubled Asset Relief Program—March 2012;* SIGTARP, *Quarterly Report to Congress,* September 30, 2010; U.S. Treasury Office of Financial Stability, *Agency Financial Report Fiscal Year 2010,* November 2010; AIG website, "What AIG Owes the U.S. Government," September 30, 2010; CRS Calculations with Fed data.

Notes: LIBOR = London Interbank Offered Rate.

a. Includes $1.6 billion in additional preferred shares issued in return for previous conversion of shares paying a mandatory dividend to shares paying an optional dividend.

TARP Housing Assistance Programs[41]

One criticism leveled in TARP's early stages was its focus on assisting financial institutions, thus providing only indirect assistance to individual homeowners facing foreclosure. Sections 103, 109, and 110 of the EESA specifically embody congressional intent that homeowners be aided under TARP. Treasury ultimately created several programs addressing this criticism. Unlike other TARP programs that have resulted in asset purchases that may eventually return some funds to the government, the housing assistance programs have no mechanism for returning funds. Some $50 billion of TARP funding was initially planned for housing assistance effort. Expected outlays under these programs have been counted as 100% spending with no expected financial return to

---

[41] For additional detail on these and other housing assistance efforts, see CRS Report R40210, *Preserving Homeownership: Foreclosure Prevention Initiatives*, by Katie Jones; portions of this section are based on this report.

the government. The amount of spending on these programs, however, has been relatively low, and the programs have been further criticized as ineffective at helping homeowners.[42]

Home Affordable Modification Program

In March 2009, the TARP Home Affordable Modification Program (HAMP) was announced.[43] Through HAMP, the government provides financial incentives to participating mortgage servicers that provide loan modifications to eligible troubled borrowers to reduce the borrowers' monthly mortgage payments to no more than 31% of their monthly income. Servicers receive an upfront incentive payment for each successful permanent loan modification and a "pay-for-success" payment for up to three years if the borrower remains current after the modification. The borrower can also receive a "pay-for-success" incentive payment (in the form of principal reduction) for up to five years if he or she remains current after the modification is finalized. Investors receive the payment cost-share incentive (that is, the government's payment of half the cost of reducing the monthly mortgage payment from 38% to 31% of monthly income), and can receive incentive payments for loans modified before a borrower becomes delinquent. Mortgage modifications can be made under HAMP until December 31, 2013.

The Administration originally estimated that HAMP would cost $75 billion. Of this amount, $50 billion was to come from TARP funds and $25 billion was to come from Fannie Mae and Freddie Mac for the costs of modifying mortgages that those entities owned or guaranteed.[44] Treasury has since revised its estimate of the amount of TARP funds that will be used for HAMP, and it has reduced the $50 billion originally allocated to HAMP to $45.6 billion and used some of those funds to help pay for other foreclosure-related programs. A total of $29.9 billion in disbursements is possible under the program, with $2.85 billion disbursed.

Hardest Hit Fund

On February 19, 2010, the Obama Administration announced that it would make funding available to the housing finance agencies (HFAs) of five states that had experienced the greatest declines in home prices. This program is known as the Hardest Hit Fund (HHF), and several additional rounds of funding, with different criteria for choosing the states, have been announced since its inception, bringing the total number of states receiving funds to 18 plus the District of Columbia. The funding comes from the TARP funds that Treasury initially set aside for HAMP. After all of the rounds of funding, the total amount of funding allocated to HHF is $7.6 billion. Of this amount, $0.9 billion has been disbursed.

---

[42] See, for example, testimony by Neil Barofsky, the Special Inspector General for TARP before the House Committee on Oversight and Government Reform, January 26, 2011, available at http://oversight.house.gov/wp-content/uploads/2012/01/Testimony.Barofsky.SIGTARP.012611.pdf.

[43] HAMP is part of the Administration's broader Making Home Affordable Program, which also includes a program to encourage refinancing of underwater mortgages backed by Fannie Mae and Freddie Mac. Funding for that program is not through TARP.

[44] November 2010 TARP 105(a) Report.

FHA Short Refinance Program

On March 26, 2010, the Administration announced a new FHA Refinance Program for homeowners who owe more than their homes are worth. Detailed program guidance was released on August 6, 2010.[45] The FHA Refinance Program is intended to use current FHA refinancing processes to include people who are underwater. Under the new program, certain homeowners who owe more than their homes are worth may be able to refinance into new, FHA-insured mortgages for an amount lower than the home's current value. The original lender will accept the proceeds of the new loan as payment in full on the original mortgage; the new lender will have FHA insurance on the new loan; and the homeowner will have a first mortgage balance that is below the current value of the home, thereby providing some equity in the home. Homeowners will have to be current on their mortgages to qualify for this program. Further, the balance on the first mortgage loan will have to be reduced by at least 10%. This program is voluntary for lenders and borrowers; however, borrowers with mortgages already insured by FHA are not eligible. The FHA Refinance Program began on September 7, 2010, and is to be available until December 31, 2014. As of the end of March 2012, FHA reported refinancing nearly a thousand mortgages through the program.[46] Treasury has committed $8.1 billion of the TARP funds originally set aside for HAMP to help pay for the cost of this program; additional program costs will be borne by FHA. Of the possible $8.1 billion, $0.06 billion has been disbursed.

Author Contact Information

Baird Webel
Specialist in Financial Economics
bwebel@crs.loc.gov, 7-0652

---

[45] FHA Mortgagee Letter 2010-23, "FHA Refinance of Borrowers in Negative Equity Positions," August 6, 2010, available at http://www.hud.gov/offices/adm/hudclips/letters/mortgagee/.

[46] Federal Housing Administration, *FHA Outlook*, March 2012, available at http://portal hud.gov/hudportal/documents/huddoc?id=ol_current.pdf.